HANDSEL

Scottish poems for
welcoming and naming babies

Handsel

*Scottish poems for
welcoming and naming babies*

Introduction by
CANDIA MCWILLIAM

Edited by
LIZZIE MACGREGOR

SCOTTISH POETRY LIBRARY
By leaves we live

Polygon

First published in 2005 by
The Scottish Poetry Library
5 Crichton's Close
Edinburgh EH8 8DT
in association with
POLYGON

ISBN 10: 1 904598 51 X
ISBN 13: 9 781904 598510

The publishers acknowledge support from
the Scottish Arts Council
towards the publication of this title.

Designed and typeset in
10/14pt Foundry Sans by James Hutcheson
Printed and bound by
The Cromwell Press, Trowbridge Wiltshire

Scottish
Arts Council
LOTTERY FUNDED

CONTENTS

It's funny when something that you remember happening quite normally crops up in a book of quaint customs. So it was when, above the entry 'Hanselling the Baby' in *Scottish Customs from the Cradle to the Grave* by Margaret Bennett, I chanced upon the custom of putting an old penny on the stump of umbilical cord on a new baby. 'Doesn't everyone do that?' I briefly thought, then remembered that I certainly hadn't, myself, with my own children, England-born and each of them not wholly Scots. It just came from the world I have come from.

How easy it is to let dear things slip. And how terribly easy it is, in the storm of business around a newborn child, and the absolute craving for sleep, deep, dreamless sleep, to forget, afterwards, exactly how it was; perhaps to forget at the time how formally to mark this new miracle, and even to forget that it is important to do so, even if the formal marking is but a recognition between father and baby, mother and baby, baby and both parents, baby and world.

That is where this book comes in. When I received a letter proposing that I might write an introduction to it, I was honoured past words. I cannot think of three words more lovely to my ear in what they represent than Scottish Poetry Library. Three things most dear to me in one place, one name. And now the poems that make up the book are here in their beauty on my desk. It is icy January out and the only flowers yet in my street are one shy hellebore and the scented blossom-on-bare-branch of viburnum. It is a perfect time to consider exactly what a handsel is.

As a noun, it's '1. a gift intended to bring good luck to something new or to a new beginning, for example the New Year, a new house or new clothes 2.(1) earnest-money, a first instalment of payment; (2) the money received by a trader for his first sale, either the first of the day or the first of a new business, thought to bring good luck 3. the first taste or experience 4. a piece of bread or other light snack given to farmworkers before beginning work.'

As a verb, it's '1. to give or offer a HANDSEL to (a person) at the beginning of a year or day, or to mark some special occasion; to present (someone) with earnest money at the beginning of an engagement 2. inaugurate with some ceremony or gift etc in order to bring good luck 3. celebrate the first use of (something) with a HANDSEL; use for the first time; be the first to try, test or taste (something)' (*The Concise Scots Dictionary*).

So, a handsel is a gift of implicit – or explicit – blessing at the start of something new, and what is newer than a new life? For the self-conscious poet, the question may be how is it possible to express afresh something that is immemorial? Especially around babies and young things, language can act soft. This book is full of terse freshnesses that see off any whiff of the sticky or of the rote. As William Soutar expresses it, in language plain as pebbles :

> Songs that the heart can share
> And understand;
> Simple as berries are
> Within the hand:

The literature of birth and infancy is, I suspect, less extensive than the literature surrounding death. Are there practical reasons for this? Is there less time around the cradle? Is everyone too tired? Have the poets absented themselves? There has perforce been a poetry of infant and premature mortality, for the double reason that it has been more common in the past than it is now, thank heaven, when there was hardly a family untouched by it, and that, in its devastating effect, it is the theft of life that most closely expresses our helplessness as humans. But the poems of simple welcome, joy or celebration, the poems of first connection, are select in number, and the collection here of high quality in that exalted few. This book constitutes a string of pearls for the telling.

There is nothing more presently real nor demandingly, hungrily, alive than a new baby. And there is nothing more suggestive of the spiritual potential we each carry. A newborn child is redemption and hope incarnate. It is, for many of us, the immanent cultural and religious metaphor with which we were raised, no matter how far from Christianity we may define ourselves as being. We are reborn through each birth among the constituency of those we love. We are offered – this time – a chance to get it right for a new soul. And the newness does not stale. This most daily of events never becomes, for even the most experienced midwife, less than miraculous.

Charms and prayers have their place here – nowhere more hopefully, of course. In addition to a poem from the Catholic poet Kathleen Raine, a long Invocation with the simplicity of heart and wildness of imagery that evoke another prayerful and practical poet, George Mackay Brown (a lovely work of whose is also here), there are prayers and charms in Scots and in Gaelic, suited to the most conventional christening or the most seagull-swooped-upon naming ceremony, open to the winds.

It is up to you to choose. I wish that I had had such a book when my children were born. A poem is like a gem at this most personally celebratory and publicly joyful of times, a compact of words and thoughts, polished for use, not only for ornament, but lovely too. It lasts longer. You can't sell it. It will not lose its value. And, while tempered, this poetry is in neither sense hard. How beautiful to read so open and unarmed (though not at all unequipped or weak) verse, for example from Aonghas MacNeacail :

a bheòil bhig
sporain nam fuaim
nad ròs réidh
's tu cala 'n t-suain

little mouth,
purse of noises
still as a rose,
now harbour of sleep

and Robert Davidson's 'Benediction'; the poem of grave beauty by
Sydney Goodsir Smith for his newborn son; Anne MacLeod's
'Evocation', which gives the baby a voice; and a lovely lucid blessing
from Scotland to a child over the Border, or maybe even further
South, from Moira Forsyth.

   Kathleen Jamie and Kate Clanchy show themselves superb
reporters from the lists of motherhood. They avoid any grudging tone
while conveying the almost ecstatic weariness of motherhood. (By
the way, I would like to make it plain here that the words that will
outlast me, for they are in the Dictionary of Quotations, that for each
child you lose two books, I never said. As accused children whine – I
never did, it's not fair. I did say that about two books' worth of effort
goes into raising a person from birth to weaning. A lot less extreme,
and not newsworthy, but I'm grateful for the opportunity to tidy that
away.)

   This little book is a seed for growing garlands to crown the fruit of
our life and of our love. These poems respond well to reading aloud.
Very probably even better to singing.

CANDIA MCWILLIAM

To the Future

He, the unborn, shall bring
From blood and brain
Songs that a child can sing
And common men:

Songs that the heart can share
And understand;
Simple as berries are
Within the hand:

Such a sure simpleness
As strength may have;
Sunlight upon the grass:
The curve of the wave.

WILLIAM SOUTAR

Evocation

First, close your eyes. Relax. Yes, I am old enough
to manage this. I've done my time

in prenatal class. Let's fix the guidelines:
I will require of you

not a degree in Quantum Physics
(uncertain as they infinitely are)

nor competence in several languages.
(One will do fine, the language of the heart.)

Singing in tune will always be a bonus
(although, if tone-deaf, do still apply)

and willingness to read, and love of story,
comforting arms, and kindness, yes: and years

years of tenderness. Oh – and a name.
I will need one of those.

Have you got all that? Let's
take it slowly. After a count of three

I'll give a cry, a short cry, not too loud.
The first of many.

Then, only then, open both your eyes
and gaze into mine.

You're ready?

ANNE MACLEOD

A Bigger World

My heart is your sun,
my blood air, food.

You float in me like Columba
in his coracle of skin;

I am your sea, walking
I rock you like waves.

I am your diving bell,
you explore on a rope

of oxygen. Shellfish
limbless you swim

until hand and foot buds
open anemone slow,

to knock, already wanting
the shore of a bigger world.

GILLIAN FERGUSON

Invocation

CHILD in the little boat
Come to the land
Child of the seals
Calf of the whale
Spawn of the octopus
Fledgeling of cormorant
Gannet and herring-gull,
Come from the sea,
Child of the sun,
Son of the sky.
Safely pass
The mouths of the water,
The mouths of night,
The teeth of the rocks,
The mouths of the wind,
Safely float
On the dangerous waves
Of an ocean sounding
Deeper than red
Darker than violet,
Safely cross
The ground-swell of pain
Of the waves that break
On the shores of the world.

Life everlasting
Love has prepared
The paths of your coming.
Plankton and nekton
Free-swimming pelagic
Spawn of the waters
Has brought you to birth
In the life-giving pools,
Spring has led you
Over the meadows
In fox's fur
Has nestled and warmed you,
With the houseless hare
In the rushes has sheltered,
Warm under feathers
Of brooding wings
Safe has hidden
In the grass secretly
Clothed in disguise
Of beetle and grasshopper
Small has laid you
Under a stone
In the nest of the ants
Myriadfold scattered
In pollen of pine forests
Set you afloat

Like dust on the air
And winged in multitudes
Hatched by the sun
From the mud of rivers.
Newborn you have lain
In the arms of mothers,
You have drawn life
From a myriad breasts,
The mating of animals
Has not appalled you,
The longing of lovers
You have not betrayed,
You have come unscathed
From the field of battle
From famine and plague
You have lived undefiled
In the gutters of cities
We have seen you dancing
Barefoot in villages,
You have been to school
But kept your wisdom.

Child in the little boat,
Come to the land,
Child of the seals.

KATHLEEN RAINE

The Birth-Bed Prayer

(Old Aberdeenshire customs)

I

It's three times roun', an' three times roun';
    Till three times three be nine: –
Gode sain this umman and hir bairn
    Wi' thy great poo'r divine:

By mornin' licht an' can'le licht –
    Fae dreids o' day an' dark –
Fae fairy wiles an' slicht o' witch,
    An' ilka care an' cark.

II

It's three times roun', an' three times roun'
    By holy can'le licht –
We pray the poo'r that sits abeen,
    To hald them in His sicht:

To keep their heids an' eke their feet
    Fae all accurs't that is
An' airt them aye the lawfu' ways
    An' grant o' grace to hiz.

III

It's three times roun', an' three times roun';
   Till three times three be nine,
Wi' book, an' breid, an' can'le licht;
   This bairn fae ill to twine: –

The bairn fae ill; the wife fae ill;
   An' hir good husband dear:
And may the poo'r that rules abeen,
   In holy love be here.

PITTENDRIGH MACGILLIVRAY

sain	*bless, protect*
umman	*woman*
poo'r	power
cark	*anxiety*
abeen	*above*
eke	*also*
airt	*direct*
hiz	*us*
twine	*keep from*

Words for my Daughter

Come, the cap of birth is dry,
my labouring is done, your cry
has split the world's roof.

Be comforted, the womb
returns to wrap around you.

Sweet darkness, velvet-blood
from which you came, as night
will cup you again, again

move you outward into light;
a brilliance to be danced in

is life. Your staggering steps
will grow to trust this earth;
it meets both sure and unsure feet.

That shifting pain will shape
the edges that define you.

Know the body that confines
is a new kind of freedom
to find the fullness of you.

Move through yourself. See,
the future is with child

and needs your labouring.
Be done with pasts, walk away.
I'll watch. I'll guard your back,

blinded by my own time. Go forward
from the shadows mothers cast.

As old women shrink, rich fruit
seeds into the garden.
I have been. Now you. So live,

we have both shed our tears
for miracles, for coming new.

In birth-sleep heavy at my breast,
love child, first comes the dream
and then the making true.

JANET PAISLEY

Setting Sail

Shock waves upended me when you
slipped the moorings
from the hull of my ribs
and my oneness became two.
Blood of my blood, bone of my bone,
your tongue salted with the same
language as my own.

When the time comes,
I will set you on the sea of life,
pick the brightest star to guide you.
Though tides may pull us
in opposite directions,
this you must promise:
never sail too far away from me.

LYDIA ROBB

Essential Relationships

'Midwives give new-born babes a small spoonfull of earth and
whisky, as the first food they taste'
        – Thomas Pennant: *A Tour of Scotland in 1769*

The bairnie greetin for the fremmit wame,
Whatna meat sall quieten him?
A wumman's breest tae warm his hert.
The barley bree tae warm his thairms.
A nip o yird tae warm his banes.

JOHN GLENDAY

fremmit	*far-off*
whatna meat	*what kind of food*
barley bree	*whisky*
thairms	*innards*
nip o yird	*taste of the earth*

Baisteadh Breith

Braon beag an Athar
  Dha do bhathais bhig, a luaidh.

Braon beag a' Mhic
  Dha do bhathais bhig, a luaidh.

Braon beag an Spioraid
  Dha do bhathais bhig, a luaidh.

Dha do chòmhnadh on a slògh,
  Dha do dhìonadh on a sluagh;

Dha do chòmhnadh on a frìd,
  Dha do dhìonadh on a fuath;

Dha do thasgadh dha na Trì,
  Dha do dhìonadh, dha do chuairt;

Dha do ghleidheadh dha na Trì,
  Dha do lìonadh le na buaidh;

Braon beag nan Trì
  Dha do lìobhadh le na buaidh.

from *Carmina Gadelica*

Birth Baptism

The little drop of the Father
    On your little brow, beloved one.

The little drop of the Son
    On your little brow, beloved one.

The little drop of the Spirit
    On your little brow, beloved one.

To save you from fairies,
    To guard you from hosting;

To keep you from elves,
    To protect you from demons;

To preserve you for the Three,
    To defend you, to enclose you;

To treasure you for the Three,
    To fill you with the graces;

The little drop of the Three,
    To make you shine with the graces.

adapted from the translation by ALEXANDER CARMICHAEL

For My Newborn Son

Blythe was yir comin
Hert never dreamt it
A new man bidan
In warld whan I've left it.

Bricht was yon morn
Cauld in September
Wi sun aa the causey
Glentered wi glamer,
Slate roofs lik siller
Schire-bleezan yon morn.

Hert in my kist lep
Joyrife its dirlan
Bairn, whan oor lips met
Yir mither's ware burnan,
Weet were oor een then
Puir words downa tell it.

As hert never dreamt on
Was joy in yir comin,
Maikless wee nesslin,
Ma sleepan reid Robin.

SYDNEY GOODSIR SMITH

blythe	*glad*
bidan	*staying*
causey	*street*
glentered wi glamer	*shone like magic*
schire-bleezan	*bright blazing*
kist	*chest*
joyrife	*joyous*
dirlan	*thumping*
maikless	*peerless*

At First, My Daughter

She is world without understanding.
She is made of sound.
She drinks me.

We laugh when I lift her by the feet.
She is new as a petal.
Water comes out of her mouth and her little crotch.

She gives the crook of my arm
A weight of delight.
I stare in her moving mirror of untouched flesh.

Absurd, but verifiable,
These words – mother, daughter –
They taste of receiving and relinquishing.

She will never again be quite so novel and lovely
Nor I so astonished.
In touch, we are celebrating

The first and last moments
Of being together and separate
Indissolute – till we are split

By time, and growth, and man,
The things I made her with.

ELMA MITCHELL

A Natal Address to My Child, March 19th 1844

Hail to thy puggy nose, my Darling,
Fair womankind's last added scrap,
That, callow as an unfledg'd starling,
Liest screaming in the Nurse's lap.

No locks thy tender cranium boasteth,
No lashes veil thy gummy eye
And, like some steak gridiron toasteth,
Thy skin is red and crisp and dry.

Thy mouth is swollen past describing
Its corners twisted as in scorn
Of all the Leech is now prescribing
To doctor thee, the newly born.

Sweet little lump of flannel binding,
Thou perfect cataract of clothes,
Thy many folds there's no unwinding
Small mummy without arms or toes!

And am I really then thy Mother?
My very child I cannot doubt thee,
Rememb'ring all the fuss and bother
And moans and groans I made about thee!

30   'Tis now thy turn to groan and grumble,
      As if afraid to enter life,
      To dare each whipping scar and tumble
      And task and toil with which 'tis rife.

      O Baby of the wise round forehead,
      Be not too thoughtful ere thy time;
      Life is not truly quite so horrid –
      Oh! how she squalls! – she can't bear rhyme!

      ELIZA OGILVY

Gift for a Newborn Child

I bring you wildflowers

gathered from the woods and moors
from seashores and lochsides
glens and meadows and the slopes of mountains

I bring you wildflowers

Little slender one   Little yellow one of the corn
Windflower   Wanderer   Lily of the glens
Cuckoo's shoe   Cat's paw   Little frog

I bring you wildflowers

Fairy's soap   Mountain silk   Soft ear
Honey plant   Milk plant   Candle of the wood
Starry stonebreaker   Flower of the lochan

I gather these for you

ELIZABETH BURNS

(Note: the words in italics are translations
of Gaelic names for wildflowers)

Observances

A boy row in a umman's coatie –
 In a man's sark row a lassie:
Nor wash their palms, nor cut their nails,
 For fear ye teem luck's tassie.

Pit breid an' cheese aneth their heids,
 An' wus them hale an' happie:
Pit butter till the bairnie's feet,
 An' syne tak' oot yer drappie.

PITTENDRIGH MACGILLIVRAY

row	*wrap up*
umman's coatie	*woman's petticoat*
sark	*shirt*
teem	*empty out*
tassie	*cup*
aneth	*beneath*
wus' them hale	*wish them healthy*
syne tak oot yer drappie	*then drink your toast*

For a Friend's Daughter Aged 1 Week

Green bud in which the flower
we may presume,
what nonchalant, unholdable power
brings you to bloom –

brings you to the brief light
of talk and caring,
which for us is blindingly bright,
sometimes past bearing –

but which yet seen more whole,
without mistaking,
is only for the roving soul
a stab at waking?

D. M. BLACK

beul beag

a bheòil bhig,
an inns' thu dhomh
nad chànan ùr
mar a lìon
do mhàthair leat –
eil cuimhn' agad

a bheòil bhig,
an seinn thu dhomh
nad chànan ùr
na h-òrain òg
a thòisich tìm

a bheòil bhig,
an dèan thu cruth
do bhiathaidh dhomh

a bheòil bhig
dé 'n cleas,
an toir thu tuar
do latha dhomh

seas, seas
a bheòil bhig,
cha tuig mi thu,
tha eas do lidean

little mouth

little mouth,
tell me
in your new language
how your mother
filled with you –
remember that?

little mouth,
sing to me
in your new language
the young songs
that started time

little mouth,
make for me
the shape of your feeding

little mouth,
what's the sport,
give me the colour
of your day

hold, hold,
little mouth,
too fast for me,
your syllables

taomadh orm
mar dhealain geal
a' sàthadh feòil chruaidh
m'fhoighidinn

a bheòil bhig
a bheòil bhig,
an ith thu mi?

a bheòil bhig,
cha tus' an aon
tha gairm do bhith

a bheòil bhig
sporain nam fuaim
nad ròs réidh
's tu cala 'n t-suain

a bheòil bhig,
nuair a thilleas tu
à gleann nam balbh
an inns' thu dhaibh
nach cual thu fòs
nad chànan ùr
nach toigh leat cràdh

AONGHAS MACNEACAIL

flood over me
in torrents of
white lightning,
stabbing the hard flesh
of my patience

little mouth,
little mouth,
would you
    eat me?

little mouth,
you're not the first
to say *i am*

little mouth,
purse of noises
still as a rose,
now harbour of sleep

little mouth,
when you return from
the dumb glen
tell those
who haven't heard
your new language
that you don't like pain

AONGHAS MACNEACAIL

Twenty Blessings

May the best hour of the day be yours.
May luck go with you from hill to sea.
May you stand against the prevailing wind.
May no forest intimidate you.
May you look out from your own eyes.
May near and far attend you.
May you bathe your face in the sun's rays.
May you have milk, cream, substance.
May your actions be effective.
May your thoughts be affective.
May you will both the wild and the mild.
May you sing the lark from the sky.
May you place yourself in circumstance.
May you be surrounded by goldfinches.
May you pause among alders.
May your desire be infinite.
May what you touch be touched.
May the company be less for your leaving.
May you walk alone beneath the stars.
May your embers still glow in the morning.

THOMAS A. CLARK

Infant

In your frowning, fugitive days, small love,
your coracled, ecstatic nights,
possessed or at peace, hands clenched
on an unseen rope, or raised in blessing
like the Pope, as your white etched feet
tread sooty roofs of canal tunnels
or lie released, stretched north in sleep –

you seem to me an early saint, a Celt,
eyes fixed on a celestial light, patiently
setting the sextant straight
to follow your godsent map, now
braced against a baffling gale, now
becalmed, fingers barely sculling
through warm muddy tides.

Soon, you will make your way out
of this estuary country, leave
the low farms and fog banks, tack through
the brackish channels and long
reed-clogged rivulets, reach
the last turn, the salt air and river mouth,
the wide grey sea beyond it.

KATE CLANCHY

Lullaby ida Mirkenin
Fae da Norwegian o Nordahl Grieg

Nicht ita da Nort is lang;
Maamie sings a sleepy-sang.
  Caald he mirkens ower da sea;
  Peerie licht – come ta me.

Caald-rife wis da day at's geen;
Sheenin blue dy boannie een
  Laek da flooer closin noo;
  Peerie licht – sleep du.

Morning brings nae sun-blink here,
Nane ava bit dee, my dear.
  By nane bit dee my hert is aesed;
  Peerie licht – waaken plaesed.

T. A. ROBERTSON (VAGALAND)

ida, ita	*in, in the*
mirkenin	*dusk*
peerie licht	*little light*
caald-rife	*very cold*
at's geen	*that's passed*
nane ava	*none at all*
dee, du	*you*

A New Child: ECL

11 June 1993

i
Wait a while, small voyager
    On the shore, with seapinks and shells.

The boat
    Will take a few summers to build
That you must make your voyage in.

ii
You will learn the names.
That golden light is 'sun' – 'moon'
    The silver light
That grows and dwindles.

And the beautiful small splinters
    That wet the stones, 'rain'.

iii
There is a voyage to make,
    A chart to read,
But not yet, not yet.
    'Daisies' spill from your fingers.
    The night daisies are 'stars'.

iv
The keel is laid, the strakes
        Will be set, in time.
A tree is growing
        That will be a tall mast.

All about you, meantime
The music of humanity,
        The dance of creation
Scored on the chart of the voyage.

v
The stories, legends, poems
Will be woven to make your sail.

You may hear the beautiful tale of Magnus
        Who took salt on his lip.
Your good angel
        Will be with you on that shore.

vi
Soon, the voyage of EMMA
        To Tir-Nan-Og and beyond.

vii
Star of the Sea, shine on her voyage.

GEORGE MACKAY BROWN

strakes   *planks*
Tir-Nan-Og   *Land of Youth*

Cradle Sang

Fa' owre, fa' owre, my hinny,
There's monie a weary airt;
And nae end to the traikin,
For man has a hungry hert.

What wud ye hae for ferlie
And no ken the want o' mair?
The sün for a gowdan aipple:
The müne for a siller pear.

WILLIAM SOUTAR

fa' owre	*go to sleep*
airt	*way*
traikin	*wandering*
ferlie	*a wonder*

Lily of Raasay

Lily of Raasay
gentle your growing
child of the islands
woodland and moor;
you will imagine
worlds for exploring
as you are stepping
over the shore.

Father and mother
comfort and hold you
their love is for you
better than gold.
Grant you courageous
sensible kindly
bonny and thoughtful
honest and bold.

Dark as the raven
eyes of the ocean
hazel and willow
wisdom and grace;
mountain and birchtrees
above and around you
light of the islands
shines from your face.

Lily of Raasay
what can I more say?
Now I behold you
give you my words.
When I have left here
they will be with you
silently singing
for all my sweet loves.

From Tessa with love for Lily in the month of May 2003

TESSA RANSFORD

(Inspired by the tune of the carol 'Child in a Manger', originally
written as 'Leonabh an Aigh' by Mary Macdonald of Bunessan;
Lily's great-grandfather was Minister of the parish of Bunessan.)

Bairnsang

Wee toshie man,
          gean tree and rowan
gif ye could staun
yer feet wad lichtsome tread
granite and saun,
but ye cannae yet staun
sae maun courie tae ma airm
an greetna, girna, Gretna Green

Peedie wee lad
          saumon, siller haddie
gin ye could rin
ye'd rin richt easy-strang
ower causey an carse ,
but ye cannae yet rin
sae maun jist courie in
and fashna, fashna, Macrahanish Sand

Bonny wee boy
          peeswheep an whaup
gin ye could sing, yer sang
wad be caller
as a lauchin mountain burn
but ye cannae yet sing
sae maun courie tae ma hert
an grieve nat at aa, Ainster an Crail

My ain tottie bairn
      sternie an lift
gin ye could daunce, yer daunce
wad be that o life itsel,
but ye cannae yet daunce
sae maun courie in my erms
and sleep, saftly sleep, Unst and Yell

KATHLEEN JAMIE

toshie	*comfy and cosy*	siller haddie	*silver haddock*
gean tree	*wild cherry*	causey	*street*
gif, gin	*if*	carse	*field*
staun	*stand*	fashna	*don't fuss*
lichtsome	*lightly*	peeswheep	*lapwing*
courie	*cuddle in*	whaup	*curlew*
greetna, girna		caller	*fresh*
	don't cry, don't fret	tottie	*tiny*
peedie	*little*	sternie an lift	*stars and sky*
saumon	*salmon*		

Benedictus

After Rabindranath Tagore

Blessins upon this wee white sowel, this hert,
Wha wins the kiss o Heiven fir oor yird;
   Wha luves the sunlicht and the face o's mither;
Nor yet looks doon his neb at common dirt,
    And bides unschuled in chasin efter siller.

Inti this laund o a hunner cross-gates
He's come, ti meet whitever here awaits:
   I ken na hou he chose you frae the thrang,
Chapped on your door, unmindful o the Fates,
    Ti follae you wi lauchter and wi sang.

Respect his trust; guide him; upon his pow
Lay a luvin haund. The waves ablow may growe
   Ti a fearsome hicht: pray that the guid braith
O Paradise sall fill his sails and rowe
    Him gentlie inti port and free o skaith.

Pit by your mony ploys, and aye caress him
Whan he coories up ti ye. He's magic. Bless him.

Scots version by TOM HUBBARD

sowel	*soul*
yird	*earth*
neb	*nose*
thrang	*crowd*
chapped	*knocked*
pow	*head*
ablow	*beneath*
skaith	*injury*
coories	*cuddles*
magic	*wonderful (West of Scotland usage)*

Collecting the Water

for Stuart and Susan Chisholm

Behind the hills November light
holds all the radiance of summer gone.
Glen Cannich blazes red and gold and green
as you dip the bottle in the burn
fill it with water clear as glass
and raise it to the sun.

I click the shutter, catch the second as it goes.

All this to bless the downy head
of a baby born to flourish
in a dry and southern soil
with the coolness of the north
the mist that veils the hills
the stillness of the loch
the translucent dusk that falls
on the land that gave him breath.

MOIRA FORSYTH

Monday's Bairn

Monday's bairn is sonsie and fair
Tuesday's bairns God's blessings bear
Wednesday's bairn wi' grief is thrang
Thursday's bairn has far ti gyang
Friday's bairn wishes a' man weel
Saturday's bairn hyows a weary dreel.
Bit the bairn that is born on the Sabbath day
Has a' the gifts a hairt could pray.

GRACE MORRISON AND PHYLLIS GOODALL

sonsie	*robust*
thrang	*familiar with*
gyang	*go (North-East)*
hyows a weary dreel	*hoes a weary drill (as in turnip drill)*

Naming

_____

your name is the print
love has made in the world,

your body the growing home
your spirit has made upon the earth,

your heart the rose
we have grown on life's stem.

Your sapling hands
hold the maker's art,

you are brother/sister to all
that crawls and walks and cries

upon the earth,
even your hair cousin to the dandelion,

your eye to bee-loving flower,
fingers to the fragile mouse –

remember in all your seasons,
you are part of the garden of the world,

shining the bottled light of us,
the best of us, which is love.

May all here present be trees,
that bending, protect you from wind,

may we be the sun
in the days and clouds of your life,

moon of your night,
smiling forever among candle stars.

Your name given here today
was written in the book of life,

only for you
as the seed dreams of light,

green and flower in every detail,
and is now spoken into the world –

_____, our child,
earth's fresh and dearest creature –

your name is the print
love has made in the world.

GILLIAN FERGUSON

'Dear Hannah'

Dear Hannah, Time no less than space
would keep us, firmly, in our place.
I being old and sluggish, here
and you, so bright and recent, there.
A here and there how far apart,
Centuries, oceans; but take heart:
that by one miracle we are
alone together on a star
and by another, that the two
I dearly love, love fondly, you.

SEÁN RAFFERTY

(Seán Rafferty's last poem; to his great-granddaughter.)

Benediction

May all your hopes be sustained
between the wings of seagulls,
and may your fears, before they start,
be taloned fast by eagles.

May curling salmon leap the falls
in the river of your strife,
and pine trees crack with age
in the forests of your life.

May speckled fawns raise their heads
beneath your vaulted blue,
and may the God of frost and stars
be ever more with you.

ROBERT DAVIDSON

On Bairns

Yeir bairns is no yeir
 bairns.
Thay ir the sons an dochters o
 Lyfe's greinin for itsell.
Thay cum throu ye, but no
 frae ye,
an tho thay byde wi ye, yit
 thay ir no yeir aucht.
Ye can gie thaim yeir luiv, but
 no yeir thochts;
for thay hae thair ain thochts.

Ye can beild thair bodies,
 but no thair sauls,
for thair sauls bydes in the houss
 o the-morn
that ye dochta veisit, no even
 in yeir dreams.
Ye can tyauve ti be lyke thaim, but seekna for
 ti mak thaim lyke you –
For Lyfe gaesna backlins nor
 daidils wi yestrein.

from *The Prophet* by KAHLIL GIBRAN
owreset intil Scots bi DAVID PURVES

greinin	*longing*
yeir aucht	*your* own
beild	*shelter*
the-morn	*tomorrow*
dochta	*cannot*
tyauve	*strive*
backlins	*backwards*
daidils	*dawdles*
yestrein	*yesterday*

Gaelic Blessing

Gun dìonadh Dia dhuibh gach bearradh,
Gum fosgladh Dia dhuibh gach bealach,
Gun rèiticheadh Dia dhuibh gach rathad,
    Agus gun gabhadh e na dhà ghlacaibh fèin sibh.

May God make safe to you each steep,
May God make open to you each pass,
May God make clear to you each road,
    And may He take you in the clasp of His own two hands.

from *Carmina Gadelica*
translated by ALEXANDER CARMICHAEL

D. M. BLACK (b.1941) was born in South Africa, and brought up in Scotland from 1950. He was most active as a poet in the 1960s and 70s; his *Collected Poems 1964–87* was published by Polygon in 1991. His translations of Goethe have appeared in *Modern Poetry in Translation*, *Chapman*, and elsewhere.

GEORGE MACKAY BROWN (1921–1996) Apart from some years in the 1950s studying at Newbattle College and at Edinburgh University, George Mackay Brown rarely left his native Orkney. His poems and stories are centred in the history and culture of the island, and reflect his concern with preserving traditions and ritual. He received an OBE in 1974, and was made a fellow of the Royal Society of Literature in 1977. The *Collected Poems* were published by John Murray in 2005.

ELIZABETH BURNS (b.1957) grew up in Edinburgh. She has published two collections of poetry, *Ophelia* (Polygon, 1991) and *The Gift of Light* (diehard, 1999), and pamphlets with Galdragon Press. Her work is also included in anthologies such as *Dream State* (Polygon, 1994 and 2002) and *Modern Scottish Women Poets* (Canongate, 2003).

ALEXANDER CARMICHAEL (1832–1912) gathered together between 1855 and 1899, largely from the Western Isles, a magnificent collection of Gaelic lore which was published as *Carmina Gadelica* (in five volumes, 1900–1954). The *Carmina* is mostly in the form of verse, with prayers, blessings, and work songs, accompanied by extensive notes and Carmichael's translations into English.

KATE CLANCHY (b.1965) Born in Glasgow, and educated in Edinburgh and Oxford, Kate Clanchy now lives in Oxford where she works as a teacher, writer and broadcaster. Her first two collections, *Slattern* (Chatto & Windus, 1995) and *Samarkand* (Picador, 1999) brought her Forward and Saltire Prizes, and her latest collection is *Newborn* (Picador, 2004), poems on birth and babies.

THOMAS A. CLARK (b.1944) was born in Greenock, spent many years in England, and has now returned to Scotland, where 'the different landscapes of the Highlands and Islands have been the central preoccupation of his poetry'. His collections include *Tormentil and Bleached Bones* (Polygon, 1993), *Distance and Proximity* (pocketbooks, 2000), and many small publications from Moschatel Press, his artist's book press in Fife.

ROBERT DAVIDSON (b.1949) is editor of the online arts magazine *Sandstone Review*. Formerly editor of *Northwords* (2001–2004), his poetry collections include *The Bird & The Monkey* (Highland Printmakers, 1995), *Total Immersion* and, as editor, *After the*

Watergaw (both Scottish Cultural Press, 1998). His book-length poem *Columba* was published in *Poetry Scotland* in 2000.

GILLIAN FERGUSON (b.1965) won a Creative Scotland Award in 2002 to explore, through poetry, the mapping of the human genome. Her second collection, *Baby* (Canongate, 2001), poems about pregnancy, birth and babies, won her a Scottish Arts Council Writer's Bursary; her most recent collection is *Chemistries* (2005). She has written for Scotland's national newspapers, and now broadcasts for BBC radio, and is media consultant for Save the Children in Scotland.

MOIRA FORSYTH (b.1951) lives and works in Ross and Cromarty. She has published short fiction, poetry, and two novels, *Waiting for Lindsay* and *David's Sisters*. She was previously fiction editor for *Northwords* magazine, and is now Fiction Director of Sandstone Press Limited.

JOHN GLENDAY (b.1952) works as an addictions counsellor for NHS Highland. In 1990 he was appointed Scottish / Canadian Exchange Fellow, and travelled widely in Canada. He was one of the founders of Blind Serpent Press. His poems have been included in many anthologies, most recently *New British Poetry* (Grey Wolf Press, 2004). Full-length publications include *The Apple Ghost* (Peterloo Poets, 1989), and *Undark* (Peterloo Poets, 1995), and he edited the bilingual anthology *La Comète d'Halcyon* (Sources, 1998).

PHYLLIS GOODALL (b.1937) has had poems published in North-Eastern magazines and anthologies since the 1990s. She and Grace Morrison worked on 'Monday's Bairn' together in a Scots language writing group in Buckie.

TOM HUBBARD (b.1950) is a librarian, poet, editor and translator, who has taught Scottish literature at universities in mainland Europe and the USA. He was Librarian of the Scottish Poetry Library 1984–1992, and Editor of the Bibliography of Scottish Literature in Translation, based at the National Library of Scotland, 2000–2004. His latest poetry publications are *From Soda Fountain to Moonshine Mountain* (Akros, 2004), and *Scottish Faust* (Kettillonia, 2004). He is an Honorary Research Fellow in the Department of Scottish Literature, University of Glasgow.

KATHLEEN JAMIE (b.1962) won the Forward Poetry Prize in 2004 for *The Tree House* (Picador, 2004). Much of her earlier poetry was collected in *Mr and Mrs Scotland are Dead: poems 1980–1994* (Bloodaxe, 2002), which was short-listed for the Griffin Poetry Prize; *Jizzen*, which includes a sequence of poems inspired by birth and motherhood, was published by Picador in 1999. Born in Renfrewshire, she studied philosophy at Edinburgh University, and now lives in Fife, teaching creative writing at St Andrews University.

PITTENDRIGH MACGILLIVRAY (1856–1938) Sculptor as well as poet, Macgillivray became a member of the Royal Scottish Academy in 1901, and was appointed King's Sculptor in Ordinary in 1921. With his lively poetry in the Scots of his native North-East, he was an early proponent of the Scottish Renaissance.

ANNE MACLEOD (b. 1951) studied medicine at Aberdeen University, and now works as a dermatologist in Inverness-shire. She is a poet and novelist, her collections of poetry being *Standing by Thistles* (Scottish Cultural Press, 1997) and *Just the Caravaggio* (Poetry Salzburg, 1999).

AONGHAS MACNEACAIL (b.1942) was born on the Isle of Skye, and brought up in a Gaelic-speaking community. He has worked in radio, film, and television, and often collaborated with musicians and artists. An active campaigner for the Gaelic language, he writes in both English and Gaelic; his collection of poems *Oideachadh Ceart / A Proper Schooling* (Polygon, 1996) won the Stakis Scottish Writer of the Year Prize.

ELMA MITCHELL (1919–2000) was born in Airdrie, and lived in London, and latterly, Somerset. She was a librarian, and also worked in publishing, and as a journalist and translator. Her *People Etcetera: poems new and selected* was published by Peterloo Poets in 1987.

GRACE MORRISON (b.1936) says she has enjoyed working on 'Monday's Bairn' with Phyllis Goodall in a Scots language writing group in Buckie.

ELIZA OGILVY (1822–1912) Born in Perth, she moved with her husband to Italy in 1848, where they became friendly with Robert and Elizabeth Browning. The 'Natal Address' was written on the day of the birth of her first child. She published several books of poetry, including the *Book of Highland Minstrelsy* (1846), in which she wove popular tales into narrative poems.

JANET PAISLEY (b.1948) grew up in central Scotland where she still lives. Her publications include five collections of poetry, the most recent being *Ye Cannae Win*, (Chapman, 2000); two of short stories; plays for theatre and radio; TV drama, and film. Her work has been widely translated. 'Words for my Daughter' is from *Alien Crop*, shortlisted for Scottish Book of the Year in 1996, and reprinted by Chapman in 2004. It was written because the poet is the mother of seven sons.

DAVID PURVES (b. 1924) was born in Selkirk, took his degrees at Edinburgh University, and followed a career as an agricultural biochemist. Dr Purves has long been an activist in the cause of the Scots language, editing the magazine *Lallans* 1987–1995. He is a prolific translator into Scots of ancient Chinese and other poetry, and has written plays in Scots, as well as his own poetry, which was published in *Hert's Bluid* (Chapman, 1995).

SEÁN RAFFERTY (1909–1993) was born in Dumfriesshire, studied at Edinburgh University, and moved to South Devon in 1948, where he ran a pub. His work was admired by Hugh MacDiarmid and Sorley MacLean. His collections are *Poems* (1999), published in two editions by etruscan and Carcanet, and *Poems, Revue Sketches and Fragments*, published by etruscan in 2004.

KATHLEEN RAINE (1908–2003) was half Scottish; the landscape of the Highlands and that of her childhood Northumbria find a place in her poetry, which largely explores the relationship between man and nature, and man and the sacred. She was a scholar and critic, the founder of *Temenos* review and the Temenos Academy, and author of numerous books of poetry; her *Collected Poems* was published by Golgonooza Press in 2000. Kathleen Raine received the Queen's Gold Medal for Poetry in 1992, and both the CBE and the Commandeur de L'Ordre des Arts et des Lettres in 2000.

TESSA RANSFORD (b.1938) worked for two decades to set up and sustain the School of Poets and the Scottish Poetry Library (before retiring at the millennium), for which services she was awarded an OBE, and spent a decade editing *Lines Review*. She continues as freelance poetry adviser and practitioner; works to encourage the publication of poetry in pamphlet form; and is active in Scottish PEN. The most recent of her eleven books of poetry is *When it Works it Feels Like Play* (Ramsay Head, 1998), and a series of pamphlet selections from Akros.

LYDIA ROBB writes poetry and prose in English and Scots. She has been published in various anthologies, including two Polygon collections of 'Shorts', and was awarded a Scottish Arts Council Writer's Bursary in 1998. Her poetry is collected in *Last Tango with Magritte* (Chapman, 2001).

T. A. ROBERTSON ('VAGALAND') (1909–1973) was brought up in Walls, Shetland, the 'Vagaland' of his poems and pen-name. Shetland was at the centre of both his life and his poetry; he taught at Lerwick Central School, and was involved in the recording of Shetland language, literature and folklore. *The Collected Poems of Vagaland* was published in 1975 by The Shetland Times.

SYDNEY GOODSIR SMITH (1915–1975) was half Scottish; born in New Zealand in 1915, he was educated in England, and studied at Edinburgh and Oxford Universities. His interest in medieval Scots led him to adopt Scots for his own work; his long love poem, 'Under the Eildon Tree' shows his mastery of the language. He also wrote a novel, *Carotid Cornucopius* (1947); his play *The Wallace* was performed at the Edinburgh Festival of 1960; and his poetry is gathered in *Collected Poems 1941–1975* (John Calder, 1975).

WILLIAM SOUTAR (1898–1943) One of the poets of the Scottish Renaissance, Soutar started to write in Scots for both adults and children in the 1920s. Having contracted an illness while in the Navy during the First World War which led to ossification of the spine, he was confined to bed for the last thirteen years of his life; this did not diminish the humour and power of his poetry. His literary output also included diaries and journals; *Into a Room: selected poems of William Soutar* (Argyll Publishing, 2000) is the most recent edition of his poetry.

ACKNOWLEDGEMENTS

Our thanks are due to the following authors, publishers, and estates who have generously given permission to reproduce works:

D.M. Black, 'For a Friend's Daughter Age 1 Week' copyright © 2005, printed by permission of the author; George Mackay Brown, 'A New Child: ECL' from *Following a Lark* (John Murray, 1996), reprinted by permission of Archie Bevan and John Murray Ltd; Elizabeth Burns, 'Gift for a Newborn' copyright © 2005, printed by permission of the author; Kate Clanchy, 'Infant' from *Newborn* (Picador, 2004), printed by permission of Macmillan, London, UK; Thomas A. Clark, 'Twenty Blessings' (Moschatel Press, 1999), reprinted by permission of the author; Robert Davidson, 'Benediction' from *Total Immersion* (Scottish Cultural Press, 1998), reprinted by permission of the author; Gillian Ferguson: 'A Bigger World' from *Baby* (Canongate, 2000), reprinted by permission of the author; 'Naming', copyright © 2005, printed by permission of the author; Moira Forsyth, 'Collecting the Water' from *Going up Ben Nevis in a Bubble Car: New Writing Scotland 18* (Association for Scottish Literary Studies, 2001), reprinted by permission of the author; John Glenday, 'Essential Relationships' (*Chapman*, No.45, 1986), reprinted by permission of the author; Tom Hubbard, 'Benedictus' copyright © 2005, printed by permission of the author; Kathleen Jamie, 'Bairnsang' from *Jizzen* (Picador, 1999), reprinted by permission of Macmillan, London, UK; Anne MacLeod, 'Evocation' copyright © 2005, printed by permission of the author; Aonghas MacNeacail, 'beul beag / little mouth' from *oideachadh ceart agus dàin eile / a proper schooling and other poems* (Polygon, 1996), reprinted by permission of Polygon Ltd; Elma Mitchell, 'At First My Daughter' from *People Etcetera: poems new and selected* (Peterloo Poets, 1987), reprinted by permission of Peterloo Poets; Grace Morrison and Phyllis Goodall, 'Monday's Bairn' copyright © 2005, printed by permission of the authors; Janet Paisley, 'Words for my Daughter' from *Alien Crop* (Chapman Publishing, 1996), reprinted by permission of Chapman Publishing; David Purves, 'On Bairns' (*Lallans* No. 39, 1992), reprinted by permission of the author; Seán Rafferty, 'Dear Hannah' from *Poems, Revue Sketches and Fragments* (etruscan, 2004), reprinted by permission of Christian Coupe; Kathleen Raine, 'Invocation' from *Collected Poems* (Golgonooza Press, 2000), reprinted by permission of Golgonooza Press; Tessa Ransford, 'Lily of Raasay' copyright © 2005, printed by permission of the author; Lydia Robb, 'Setting Sail' copyright © 2005, printed by permission of the author; T.A. Robertson, 'Lullaby ida Mirkenin' from *Collected Poems of Vagaland* (Shetland Times, 1975), reprinted by permission of Mrs Martha Robertson; Sydney Goodsir Smith, 'For My Newborn Son' from *Collected Poems 1941–1975* (John Calder, 1975), reprinted by permission of Calder Publications UK Ltd; William Soutar, 'To the Future' and 'Cradle Sang' from *Poems of William Soutar: a new selection* (Scottish Academic Press, 1988), reprinted by permission of the Trustees of the National Library of Scotland.